The Three Holy Kings of Cologne

The Three Holy Kings of Cologne

How They Journeyed From Persia to Cologne and Their Veneration in England

HUGH MOUNTNEY

GRACEWING

First published in 2003

Gracewing
2 Southern Avenue, Leominster
Herefordshire HR6 0QF

ISBN 0 85244 407 9

Half title page illustration:
Pilgrim's Badge, the Gemeente-Museum,
Nijmegen.

Cover Illustration:
Stained glass window, *The Magi Journeying to Bethlehem*,
by kind permission of the Dean and Chapter, Canterbury.

Typeset by Action Publishing Technology Ltd,
Gloucester GL1 5SR

Printed by Antony Rowe Ltd,
Eastbourne BN23 6QT

Contents

Acknowledgements

Amongst those who have helped me in this research, I must first express my grateful thanks to my son, William, who by internet not only discovered important information about various sources which enabled him to locate out-of-print books and have them sent from far corners of the earth, but also typed out the whole work for me. I am indebted to Miss Suzanne Eward, Librarian of Salisbury Cathedral, for information about the medieval representation of the Adoration there as well as copies of parts of the Sarum Liturgy. I am grateful to Miss Townsend of the Victoria and Albert Museum, who sent me a photocopy of a pilgrim's badge. I should like too to thank Mr Matt Cambridge, Research Curator of Nottingham Castle Museum and Art Gallery for producing copies of W. L. Hildburgh's article in *Art Bulletin* and a similar article by Clement Pitman in *The Connoisseur*.

Two other members of my family have assisted: daughter Alison who photographed and obtained information about the Bristol Almshouse, and daughter-in-law Anthea, who supplied information about the carving in Kirknewton Church.

I am grateful to the Trustees of the National Museums of Scotland for the use of the photograph of The Adoration of the Magi from the Franciscan Friary, Dundee, and to Luthe Verlag, Cologne, who kindly gave their permission for the use of the photograph of the Three Kings Shrine in Cologne Cathedral.

O Almighty Creator of the Heavens, who revealed thy incarnation by the testimony of a bright heavenly star, which seeing, the Magi adored thy Majesty with the offering of gifts: in thanksgiving therefore, I offer to thee the sacrifice of praise and graciously beseech thee to grant to me that in my mind the star of righteousness may always appear, and that my treasure may be confessing thee, Lord Jesus Christ. Amen.

Prayer from the Book of Cerne, compiled in Mercia, in the early ninth century.

Introduction

Hugh Mountney

Of recent years, Christmas cards which illustrate the Nativity of Our Lord have increasingly been displaced by pictures, sometimes burlesque, of the Three Kings. This is no doubt commerce's reaction to sales in a pluralistic society, to avoid showing the fundamental reason for celebrating Christmas, the Incarnation of the second Person of the Trinity. But it is true that the story of the Three Kings has always gripped people's imagination.

In 1975, I became chaplain to the British Embassy in Bonn with a church and congregation in Cologne as well, and on 6 January 1977, we went on a second visit to the Dom (cathedral) there. It was a very sleety journey up the autobahn from Bonn, and it was an exciting experience to emerge from the underground car park into the Dom Platz and see the enormous church flood-lit. Looking up to the two spires, we could see the lovely tracery and windows of the towers, dark grey and white as the snow flakes drifted down. It was quite ethereal.

It is impossible to describe the vastness of this church. It is not only its length – one always seems miles away from the high altar – but also its enormous height. There were candles everywhere, not only on the altar but also around the clerestory at the far end of the chancel. Inside, a huge congregation had assembled in bitter cold. Every seat was taken in the nave and the aisles were full of folk who were standing. Then Mass was sung. As the consecration drew near, the huge deep-toned bell in the tower began to toll in a most solemn manner, and continued throughout the words of institution. After communion, a procession was formed and the whole congregation followed the sacred ministers and robed members of various brotherhoods to the east end of the chancel, where in a magnificent shrine lie the bones of the Three Kings, and prayers were said. We are not in the Middle Ages. Here is a country of advanced scientific knowledge, and still hundreds of people venerate the Three Kings.

Nor are they forgotten after the Mass. During Epiphanytide, there is held a special service of the 'Sternsinger' – 'star singers'. Groups of three children dressed in eastern clothes – one with a black face, led by an angel carrying a star on a pole – come to the cathedral for a service of hymns, prayers and an address. Then the Archbishop blesses the Sternsingers and also pieces of chalk, a piece being given to each group. During the following evenings, the Sternsingers go round the streets, stopping at each house to sing Three Kings' hymns. They receive gifts of money to be sent to the needy in distressed parts of the world, and mark each door with the blessed chalk – C M B – Casper, Melchior, Balthazar – together with the year's date.

As a result of these experiences, I wanted to know how the bones of the Three Kings came to Cologne. Through my son who worked in the University Bookshop in Bonn, I was able to borrow from the University Library (and later purchase a copy of) a recently published book *Die Heilige Drei Könige* by Hans Hofmann, a thorough and painstaking research of the subject.

Hans Hofmann refers to the tradition that Helena, mother of the Emperor Constantine, made a pilgrimage in the fourth century to the Holy Land. After building churches on the sites of the Nativity, Crucifixion and Burial of Our Lord, she wished to find the bones of the Three Kings. She set out on a journey into the East, and eventually discovered them. She had the bones put into a marble coffin and presented it to the great Church of Sancta Sophia in Constantinople.

In the middle of the fourth century, Eustorgius, as the Emperor's counsellor and ambassador, visited Milan and was chosen by the people as their bishop, subject to the Emperor's consent. He agreed and presented Eustorgius with the bones of the Three Kings. Eustorgius brought them to Milan and built a church where they were laid to rest.

Here, a monk of Malmesbury, Wiltshire, writing in 1366 can take up the story: 'In 1158 the bodies of the Three Magi were discovered, unimpaired from corruption, in a certain old chapel near the town of Milan, and reburied in the city'. William, an Augustinian canon of Newburgh Priory, Yorkshire, writing in *Historia Anglicana* continues: 'At that time (1164) Friederic Barbarossa besieged, took and overthrew Milan ... The Milanese fortified themselves with all their power against the imperial assault ... When the suburbs were demolished, lest they should be put to evil use, both the monastery and the precious honourable remains of saints, which were outside the walls, they took into the city, particularly the bodies of the Three Magi ... That treasure, once secretly placed in the church, lay hidden to the monks ... but when the church was pulled down to its foundations, it was discovered and proved by clear signs ... that these men, whose memory is blessed, having honoured and adored the Saviour returned home ... These relics had the skin, though dried and incorrupt, with bones and nerves, preserved by the action of balsam, with which bodies after death were anointed according to Gentile customs ... When the victorious Emperor overthrew the city ... he transferred the relics to the kingdom of Germany, and distinguished the city of Cologne with the care of this treasure. The Emperor gave the relics to his Chancellor, the Archbishop of Cologne, Reinald von Dassel.'

It is uncertain which route Reinald took back to Cologne. There exists a whole string of shrines purporting to mark the places where the relics rested for a night on their way over the Alps, but as these altars and chapels only go back to the fourteenth and fifteenth centuries, they do not provide proof, especially as travellers invoked the patronage of the Three Kings when going on a journey. (See the text of the Itinerarium, p. 17.)

There are important traditions that Reinald took his journey through Burgundy – there is an early reference to the cult of the Three Kings at the Cistercian Abbey of Lieu-croissant; at Estrabonne between Besançon and Dôle there is a spring known as *Fons Trium Regum*; in a very old chapel near Bellières and in many other places around Besançon traces exist.

After leaving Burgundy, Reinald reached the Rhein at Breisach. In return for the hospitality he received there, he presented the people with the bones of St Gervasius. But next day, the boat in which he was travelling refused to leave, and Reinald remembered that the brothers Gervasius and Protasius were reported by St Ambrose as not wishing to be parted – even by death. The way out of this impasse was to give the bones of St Protasius to the people of Breisach as well.

The Archbishop probably stopped at Mainz, for there is a house chapel there, in the old Truckhaus, dedicated to the Three Kings. In a splendid side room, known as the Kings' Chamber, the Three Kings rested for the night. At Remagen, he paused again, for the boat suddenly stopped. There he had to leave the bones of St Apollinaris, which were enshrined in the sixth-century chapel of St Martin on the hill side, and then the journey continued.

After three years' absence, Reinald von Dassel arrived in Cologne in July 1164 – some say on 24 July, the vigil of St James, others on 23 July, which is more probable as the liturgy of the Kölner Dom (Cologne Cathedral) from the second half of the twelfth century gives this date, and it is still kept as the Feast of the Translation of the Three Kings.

The relics were taken in procession with hymns and psalms through the Königs-pforte (King's Gate) to the

Cathedral. In 1181, Nicolaus of Verdun began the construction of a wonderful shrine, and in 1190 it was placed behind the high altar where it remains to this day. Cologne developed into one of the great pilgrimage centres of Christendom, being the most visited after Jerusalem, Rome, Santiago and Aachen. Around 1300, the stream of pilgrims from England (including King Edward II and King Edward III), Spain, Italy, and France never stopped.[1]

As late as the early seventeenth century, Thomas Coryate, son of the rector of Odcombe in Somerset, was a pilgrim at Cologne, and in 1608 published a translation of Johannes von Hildesheim's *Three Holy Kings*.

Are the bones in the shrine at Cologne really those of the Three Magi – 'Wise Men' – who were probably astrologers? It was not until the third century that they were called 'Kings'. The earliest reference to that title is in Tertullian, who based it on Psalm 72 verse 10: 'The Kings of Tharsis and of the isles shall bring presents: the Kings of Arabia and Saba shall bring gifts. All kings shall fall down before him, and all nations shall do him service.'

When the coffin was opened in 1864, within were found the remains of a young man, a man of middle age, and an old man. In 1981 Professor David de Jonghe, an international expert on the provenance of ancient materials, examined some small fragments of their clothes which had been taken out in 1864 and preserved in the Diocesan Museum. He maintains that they were made from antique damask, which in the period between the second and the fourth centuries was woven in the Near East and was not made after that time. It is similar to cloth found in a tower in Palmyra dating from AD 103–272. It has the same number of threads; the direction of the warp and weft and the turn of the yarn are the same; the weft threads are of wool covered with real purple, i.e. dye made from thousands of molluscs (*Murex purpuridae*), with gold working. Such material was the symbol that the wearer was of the highest rank.

While the Three Kings came to be enshrined in Cologne, devotion to them in Northern Europe goes back a long time before 1164, even in England.

The church of Kirknewton in Northumberland has a stone sculpture of the Three Magi, which appears to have been made before the ninth century. Various details have led scholars to favour an earlier date – the haloes emerge from the shoulders of the Magi and they wear kilts, and Phrygian caps similar to those on the Magi in the *Capella Greca* in the catacomb of St Priscilla in Rome, *c.*AD 200. It has been suggested that the sculptor may have been given instructions by Bishop Paulinus or St James the Deacon, who came from Italy and preached in Northumberland, and who might have known the painting in the catacomb or the mosaic in Ravenna, *c.*547. Possibly the carving was made for King Edwin's chapel at his country seat at Yeavering (Adgefryn) a few miles away, where Paulinus baptized. Another early reference to devotion to the Three Kings in England occurs in the Benedictional of St Aethelwold, Bishop of Winchester at the end of the tenth century, which has no less than three blessings mentioning the Magi for the Feast of the Epiphany in addition to the collect for the day.

In Scotland there is the (now) restored shrine of the Three Kings in the episcopalian north aisle (the burial place of the Earls of Lauderdale) of the parish kirk of Haddington, originally given by David Forrest in 1522.

At Thetford Priory in Norfolk there had been a stone sculpture of the Three Kings in the north chapel, which had been the burial place of the Dukes of Norfolk. The sculpture is now to be found in St Peter Hungate museum in Norwich.

Looking for any liturgical references to the Three Kings, apart from the Mass reference to them at Epiphany, the Sarum Missal provides for a Mass 'Pro itinerantibus de sanctis tribus Regibus Coloniae' (Travellers' Mass of the Three Kings at Cologne). There had been a brilliantly painted and moving carving of the Three Kings at Salisbury Cathedral, described by two travellers from the continent, in 1465.[2] They were a Czech, Vaclav Sasek and a German, Gabriel Tetzel, companions of Leo von Rozmital, who spent two years touring Europe. Sasek wrote: 'I have never seen more beautiful statues anywhere. One represents the Virgin holding the Christchild in her arms and the Three Kings bring presents ... It is executed in such a manner that it appears not that it has been carved out of wood, but as if it were alive and the events were taking place before your very eyes.' And Tetzel adds: 'We saw some fine figures which were so worked with weights that they moved as if to show how the Three Kings brought gifts to our Lady and her Babe, how our Lord reached out to take the gifts, and how our Lady and St Joseph bowed and did obeisance to the Three Kings and how they took their leave.'

It is interesting in view of this shrine in Salisbury Cathedral that the Bishop of Salisbury at the Council of Constance, 1414–18, saw a presentation of the Dreikönigsspiel (Three Kings' Play, which was begun in the twelfth century in Cologne) on 24 January and on Candlemas Day in 1417, to which the English bishops had been invited.

There is a chapel, dedicated to the Three Kings of Cologne, in Bristol. At the top of Christmas Steps, Colston Street, stands Foster's Almshouse, which was built by John Foster, a wealthy salt merchant who was Sheriff of Bristol in 1474, Mayor in 1481, and Member of Parliament in 1489. His business took him to the continent and he traded in the Rhineland. Cologne merchants were the earliest and specially privileged German merchants in England; they themselves and their wares and their own Market Hall, The Guildhall, were taken into particular protection by King Henry II in 1157. This was the beginning of three hundred years of particular protection for these Hanseatic merchants in England. No wonder that such a one as John Foster was familiar with Cologne. He must have seen the magnificent reliquary containing the remains of the Three Kings, for when he founded the Almshouse in 1484 he had the chapel dedicated to the

Three Kings of Cologne. The Almshouse and chapel were built on a parcel of land in the demesne of the Abbot of Tewkesbury who had jurisdiction over parts of the city of Bristol at that time, and he had to have the abbot's permission for that dedication. At the restoration of the chapel in 1962, modern statues of the Three Kings replaced those destroyed at the Reformation in the niches on the exterior of the east end of the chapel, and stained glass windows portraying them were installed in the east windows. Inside there are medieval floor tiles with the letters C M B (Casper, Melchior, Balthazar) and stars are set in the barrel vault above.

E. Carus Wilson in *Die Hanse* writes 'Another English export article ... were sculptures of high quality prepared from English alabaster in Nottingham, York and other places, and were very much in demand on the continent.'[3] Those surviving also provide evidence for the cult of the Three Kings.

Over 100 panels of the Adoration have survived. In the earliest fourteenth-century panels, the details have been standardized. In the ten recorded examples of this early type, all are of the Nativity combined with the Adoration of the Magi. In the fourteenth century this combination of Nativity and Adoration seems to have been a particular favourite in England: '... there are many hundreds of fragments of alabaster panels and figures discovered in England under floors, in the walls and in the roofs of churches, and less frequently, of houses, which leaves no doubt that there was a thriving home market.'[4]

There were two forms of alabaster groups of figures, broad ones combining the Nativity with the Adoration of the Kings, and tall ones, displaying either the Five Joys of Mary or incidents in the Lord's Passion, or single figures. The carving of alabaster for devotional purposes as distinct from placing on monuments or as a reredos dates from 1340–45. Those of the Nativity with the Magi were intended for use by themselves, and not in sets to be placed behind an altar. 'It should be remembered that the

Nativity combined with the Adoration of the Kings is decidedly more likely to have been presented in isolation than most scenic subjects. Not only does it involve ... a representation of our Lady with the Infant Christ, but it also honours the Three Kings whose powerful guardianship it might well have been prepared to invoke and perhaps – even through simulation of their actual presence – to have secured.'[5]

It is recorded that 'in September 1550, the English Ambassador to France complained of three or four ships having lately arrived from England, unloading images in Paris and Rouen'. This of course was the result of the violence of the Puritans, who threw them out of churches with other works of art.

Eammon Duffy comments in *The Stripping of the Altars*:

> The Three Kings of Cologne, directly led by God ... were frequently invoked as intercessors and protectors. Their names often occur in incantatory prayers for deliverance from evil, and they were invoked as protectors against bites of mad dogs or the falling sickness ... Prayers to them were an invariable element in the small group of morning prayers in most Books of Hours.

The Hereford Municipal Archives record the feast of Corpus Christi in 1503, when pageants went through the town in which the Guild of Tailors' scene was 'The Three Kings of Colen' (Cologne).

Up to Vatican II an *Itinerarium* (form of prayer for travellers) was included in the Roman Breviary. One of the prayers is '*Deus qui filios Israel per maris medium sicco vestigio ire fecisti, quique tribus Magi iter ad te stella duce pandisti: tribus nobis iter prosperum ...*'. (see p. 17).

The Victoria & Albert Museum in London houses the largest alabaster collection in the world and includes 200 pieces donated to the museum by W. L. Hildburgh. In the catalogue[7] ten of the illustrations are of the Adoration of the Magi. In the Museum of London there is also a pilgrim badge from the shrine of the Three Kings of Cologne which had been found in England, pointing to the fact that English people went to Cologne on pilgrimage.[8] I discovered that there had been an alabaster of the Three Kings at West Barsham church, Norfolk, probably originally from Castle Acre priory, but it was recently stolen from the church. At Long Melford in Suffolk, I saw and photographed a wonderful alabaster of the Adoration of the Magi, dating from 1350, which was dug up from beneath the chancel floor in the eighteenth century, probably buried there by the family of Cloptons, to protect it from the destruction of the Puritans. There are others in this country, e.g. in St Laurence's church, Reading, Treslothian church in Cornwall, now on loan to the Royal Cornwall Museum, Truro, and in Stoneyhurst College.

A very interesting piece of evidence to the devotion given to the Three Kings in this country is a ceremony still performed to this day by royalty, begun in the fifteenth century. In the Chapel Royal at St James's Palace on the Feast of the Epiphany every year, the English monarch joins the Magi in offering the Christ Child the gifts of gold, frankincense and myrrh. Until the eighteenth century, the monarch usually attended the ceremony in person, but today the offerings are made on the sovereign's behalf by two Gentlemen Ushers of the monarch in the presence of a detachment of the Yeomen of the Guard. Frankincense and myrrh are provided by the Apothecary of the monarch and afterwards given to the Church. Gold, consisting of five gold sovereigns (lent by the Bank of England) are offered, and an equivalent sum given to charity.[9]

To show how much the Three Kings were remembered in the popular mind, one could mention public houses. There is a Three Kings Inn at Fornham All Saints in Suffolk, with a sign depicting them on their way to Bethlehem; another at Heydon in Norfolk; several large signs in the Guildhall Museum in London; one at Aston-under-Hill and a fifteenth-century one at Hanley Castle,

Worcestershire. In Norwich there is a Three Kings lane where once there was an inn of that name. At Mitcham, Surrey, there is held a Fair on the Three Kings Common on 12–14 August each year near to an inn of that name. No doubt inns called The Star or The Crown originally referred to the Three Kings.

Another custom, which still continues in English life and is derived from the Three Kings, is the content of Christmas crackers: paper crowns, gifts and mottos probably representing the prophecy of the star arising out of Jacob, which foretold the birth of the King.

Hans Hofmann mentions only four places in Britain under the patronage of the Three Kings: Cotehele House, Cornwall with a triptych behind the altar, 1589; Dundee, a Chaplaincy to St Mary and the Three Kings of Cologne, founded in 1517 by Bishop George Brown, with a carving in the chapel, now in the Scottish Museum of Antiquities, Edinburgh; Haddington described above p. 6; Aberdeen, a reredos of the Three Kings, presented to the parish kirk of St Nicholas by King Robert III (1390–1406), now in the chapel of the Blessed Virgin. He also mentions a painting in St Stephen's chapel, Westminster Palace depicting the Three Kings with King Edward III and his five sons. The chapel is now demolished, but pictures of this window have survived and are reproduced in Borenius/Tristram *English Paintings*. Maurice in his book on St Stephen's chapel (Cambridge, 1955) mentions a William Partington's making images in 1351 'of three kings to stand in the tabernacles', with a footnote 'Possibly the Three Kings of Cologne'. As both Edward II in 1322 and Edward III in 1338 made pilgrimages to the Shrine at Cologne, the latter giving 58 shillings and six pennies, this seems very likely.

Perhaps the most important evidence of devotion to the Three Kings of Cologne are two literary witnesses to the fact that the English were quite familiar with the Shrine at Cologne.

The first is the Golden Legend by Jacobus de Voragine, 1275, which was translated into English by Caxton in 1470.

There it is stated that 'the bodies of the Three Kings were brought to Milan (where as now is the convent of the friars preachers), and now be at Cologne in St Peter's church, which is the Cathedral and See of the Archbishop', (at the end of chapter 'Feast of the Epiphany') (see pp. 19, 20).

The second is even more conclusive. In *c*.1370 Johannes von Hildesheim wrote *Historia Trium Regum*, a legendary account of all the biblical events which preceded the visit of the Three Kings to the Christ Child, beginning with the prophecy of Balaam in Numbers 24, 17: 'there shall come a star out of Jacob, and a sceptre shall rise out of Israel'. This was translated into English, and the fact that many manuscripts of the fifteenth century are still extant, and several printed versions by Wynkyn de Worde, Caxton's successor, of 1499, 1511, 1526 and 1530 still exist, show that it was well known. This is further concrete evidence that devotion to the Three Kings of Cologne was widespread in England, and no doubt we again have to thank the excesses of the Puritans for the fact that most shrines were demolished at the Reformation.

According to C. Horstmann, who edited the medieval English text of the *Historia Trium Regnum* in 1886, Johannes von Hildesheim was born at Hildesheim. He was a Carmelite friar, who studied at Avignon and became a doctor of Divinity there. In 1358, he was appointed 'Biblicus' in Paris. He returned to Germany and became prior at Cassel, from where he was sent on a mission to Rome in 1366. On his return he was made prior of the Convent of Marienau where he died in 1375. He wrote a number of books in addition to the *Historia* which was a great success.[10]

With his wide contacts, he could have come across Marco Polo's *Travels* which was translated into many languages. In 1271, Marco Polo, with his father and uncle, travelled to China, and during his stay there was sent by Kublai Khan as an envoy and ambassador to Yunnan, Burma, Cochin China and India. The three travellers returned to Venice in 1295 via Sumatra, India and Persia.

Marco mentions sepulchres of three Magi, who had journeyed to worship a child with gifts of gold, frankincense and myrrh (see p. 22).

There are numerous copies of Johannes' work in German libraries. There are two Latin manuscripts in Cologne, three in Bamberg, one in Munich, and one in Utrecht. Printed Latin versions – five in Cologne and one in Bamberg. German manuscripts – one in Fulda, one in Munich, one in Heidelberg and three in Cologne, with five printed editions in Cologne, according to Elisabeth Christern, who published a German translation from the Latin printed version of 1477 by Johann Guldenschaff in Cologne.

My attention was drawn to the *Historia* of Johannes von Hildesheim by a facsimile of Karl Simrock's edition of 1842, published in 1979 for the occasion of the centenary of the completion of the building of Cologne Cathedral. This original edition of 1842 was instigated by Goethe. He spent a few weeks in Jena in 1839 when he took out some old manuscripts from the town library. Amongst them he found a manuscript of 'The Legend of the Three Kings of Cologne' by Johannes von Hildesheim. He encouraged his friend Gustav Schwab to make a German translation in 1822 from a version of the Latin in Goethe's handwriting and a German version in the Heidelberg library. This I have translated into English.

The English manuscript versions are full of additional matter of legendary character, which was inserted by various translators, and in a colophon of Wynkyn de Worde's 1530 printed edition, there occurs the following: 'This was brought into Englysshe of an olde translacyon, rugh and rude, and required to amend it. I thought lesse labour to wryte new the whole'. Who made the first translation from the Latin into English is not known, but the Ashmolean manuscript states: 'Translated oute of latyne into Englisshe by the grettest doctours of our nacioun, licenced by the church'. It would therefore appear to be better to print my English translation of the German version by Schwab, which is closer to the Latin original.

Notes

1. Cf. Walter Schulten, *Der Schrein der Heiligen Drei Königen.*
2. Information from the Cathedral Librarian, Salisbury.
3. E. Carus Wilson in *Die Hanse.*
4. Francis Cheetham in *English Medieval Alabaster.*
5. W. H. Hildburgh in *Art Bulletin.*
6. Francis Cheetham in 'Gothic Export', *Antique Collector*, 1993.
7. Francis Cheetham, *English Alabaster Sculptures.*
8. Information from Miss E. Townsend, assistant curator, Victoria & Albert Museum.
9. Neil Macgregor, *Seeing Salvation.*
10. C. Horstmann (ed.), *Historia Trium Regnum.*

The Sarum Missal

In the Cathedral Library at Salisbury, there is a reprint of the *Missale ad usum insignis et praeclarae Ecclesiae*, SARUM, 1861, containing 'Missa pro itinerantibus de sanctis tribus Regibus Coloniae'. Also there is a copy of *Missale Romani Mediolani*, Milan, 1474, which also contains a Mass 'De tribus Magis'. The use of Sarum was the most popular in England, so that this Mass would not be restricted to that diocese.

The following are the prayers to be used; while the Office, Epistle, Gradual, Alleluya, Gospel, Offertory and Communion sentences are those of the Epiphany.

Collect

O God, who led by a star the three eastern Magi, Jasper, Melchior and Balthazar, to thy cradle, to venerate thee with mystical gifts; we beseech thee that by the devout prayers of these Three Kings thou wouldest grant to thy servants N. gladness, grace and peace that in the journey they are undertaking they may be led by the true sun, the true star and true light of lights to the place they intend in peace and safety and when their business is completed may return with all prosperity, in health and safety:
Who livest & reignest.

Secret

Receive, most merciful God, the oblations which we offer to thee, the living and true God, in thy honour and in the solemn commemoration of thy blessed Three Kings and Magi, Jasper, Melchior and Balthazar; that through this holy sacrifice and their glorious prayers thou wouldest free us from all snares of our enemies, and deliver us from all dangers of this world, and bring us to eternal joys. Through our Lord.

Post Communion

May the glorious intercession of thy Three Holy Kings and Magi, Jasper, Melchior and Balthazar, we beseech thee, O Lord, protect and assist us everywhere; and through these holy sacraments which we have received absolve us from the chains of our sins, and evermore protect us and defend us from all enemies, and vouchsafe to lead us to thy presence. Through our Lord.

[My translation of the Latin.]

ITINERARIUM – Prayers to be said before a journey

After the Benedictus and versicles and responses:

Deus, qui filios Israel per maris medium sicco vestigio ire fecisti, quique tribus Magi iter ad te stella duce pandisti: tribue nobis, quaesumus, iter prosperum tempusque tranquillum; ut, Angelo tuo sancto comite, ad eum quo pergimus locum, ac demum ad aeternae salutis portum pervenire feliciter valeamus.

> God who madest the children of Israel to go dryshod in the midst of the sea, and who shewedst to the Wise Men the way unto thyself by the leading of a star; grant unto thy servants, we beseech thee, a prosperous journey and a quiet time, that attended by thy holy Angel, we may safely reach the place whither we would go, and at length attain to the haven of eternal salvation.

Evidently the idea that the Three Kings were patrons of travellers had not died out by the seventeenth century in England. In his book *Private Prayers*, Bishop Lancelot Andrewes has these prayers 'Before a Journey':

Send me good speed this day;
if thy presence go not with me, carry me not up hence.
Thou who didst speed the way
of Abraham's servant by the leading of an angel:
of the Wise Men by the leading of a star:
. . . be with me, O Lord, and speed my way:
bring me to my journey's end,
and bring me home again.

William Laud, who became Archbishop of Canterbury in 1633, also has an Itinerary in his book of Private Devotions.

> O Domine, stellam ducem non sum
> meritus, tribue tamen, quaesao,
> mihi iter prosperum, tempus tranquillum,
> reditum felicem. Ut angelo
> tuo sancto comite et custode, ad
> eum quo pergo locum, deinde ad
> domum propriam, et demum ad
> aeternae salutis portum, pervenire
> feliciter valeam. Per Jesum
> Christum Dominum nostrum.

(Translation)

> O Lord, I am not worthy of the leading of
> a star, but grant to me, I beseech thee,
> a prosperous journey, a peaceful time, a
> happy return: so that with thy holy angel
> as my companion and guardian I may be worthy
> to reach the place whither I go, then my
> own home and at the last the haven of
> eternal salvation. Through Jesus Christ
> our Lord.

The Golden Legend

A very popular book in the Middle Age was the *The Golden Legend* by Jacobus de Voragine, 1275, Archbishop of Genoa. This was a commentary on the seasons of the Church's year, accounts of the patriarchs of the Old Testament and lives of the saints. It was translated into English and printed by Caxton in 1470 – no other books were reprinted as many times between 1470 and 1530.

Voragine writes: 'The Feast of the Epiphany of our Lord is adorned with four miracles and after them it hath four names. On this day the Kings worshipped Jesus Christ and St. John Baptist baptised him. And Jesus Christ changed the water into wine and he fed five thousand men with five loaves of bread ...'

'When Jesus Christ was thirteen days old the Three Kings came to him the way like as the star led them, and therefore this day is called Epiphany. ... The Three Kings came from far countries and the Jews were neighbours fast by. These Kings were successors of Balaam and came to the vision and sight of the star by the prophecy of their fathers, which said that a star shall be born or spring out of Jacob, and a man shall arise out of the lineage of Israel.'

(There follows the scriptural account of their asking the way of Herod, their offering of the three gifts, with a spiritual meaning to each as described by St John Chrysostom, St Austin and St Jerome.)

'And the Kings when they were admonished and

warned by revelation in their sleep that they should not return by Herod, and by another way they should return to their country, lo, hear how they came and went in their journey. For they came to adore and worship the King of kings in their proper persons, by the star that led them, and by the prophet that enseigned and taught them. And by the warning of the angel returned and rested at their death in Jesus Christ. Of whom the bodies were brought to Milan, where as now is the convent of the friars preachers, and now be at Cologne in St Peter's Church which is the Cathedral and See of the Archbishop.'

Marco Polo

The following excerpt from what Marco Polo found in Persia is interesting for his mention of the Three Kings and the similarity to some of the details in Johannes von Hildesheim's *Historia*:

'In Persia is the city of Saba, from which the three Magi set out when they went to worship Jesus Christ; and in the city they are buried in three very large and beautiful monuments, side by side ... The bodies are still entire, with the hair and beard remaining. One of these was called Jasper, the second Melchior and the third Balthasar. Messer Marco asked a great many questions of the people of that city as to those Three Magi, but never one could he find that knew aught of the matter, except that these were three kings who were buried there in days of old. However, at a place three days' journey distant ... he found a village which goes by the name of Cala Ataperistan, which is as much as to say "The Castle of the Fire-worshippers" ... for the people do worship fire. They relate that in old times three kings of that country went away to worship a Prophet that there was born, and they carried with them three manner of offerings, Gold and Frankincense, and Myrrh; in order to ascertain whether that Prophet were God, or an earthly King, or a Physician. For, said they, if he take the Gold, then he is an earthly King; if he take the Incense he is God; if he take the Myrrh he is a Physician.

'So it came to pass when they had come to the place where the Child was born ... they agreed to go in all three together, and on doing so they beheld the Child with the appearance of its actual age, to wit, some thirteen days. Then they adored, and presented their Gold and Incense and Myrrh. And the Child took all the three offerings, and then gave them a small closed box; whereupon the Kings departed to return into their own land.

'And when they had ridden many days they said they would see what the Child had given them. So they opened the little box, and inside it they found a stone. On seeing this they began to wonder what this might be that the Child had given them, and what was the import thereof. Now the signification was this: when they presented their offerings, the Child had accepted all three, and when they saw that, they had said within themselves that He was the True God, and the True King, and the True Physician. And what the gift of the stone implied was that this Faith which had begun in them should abide as firm as a rock. Howbeit, they had no understanding at all of this signification of the gift of the stone, so they cast it into a well. Then straightaway a fire from Heaven descended into that well wherein the stone had been cast.

'And when the Three Kings beheld this marvel they were sore amazed, and it greatly repented them that they had cast away the stone; for well they perceived that it had a great and holy meaning. So they took of that fire, and carried it into their own country, and placed it in a rich and beautiful church. And there the people keep it continually burning, and worship it as a god, and all the sacrifices they offer are kindled with that fire.'

In 1986, William Dalrymple followed the route taken by Marco Polo to China, and stopped at Saveh. This town was in ruins, but he discovered later in the *Chronicle of Khazwim* that there had been a building there full of astronomical instruments, globes and telescopes. This could well have been the headquarters of the Magi. 'Magi' is the Persian name for the ancient Zoroastrian priestly fire worshippers.

The Zoroastrians believed in the coming of a messiah whose birth would be announced by a bright star. Recent research by Adrian Gilbert in *Magi: the quest for a secret tradition* and Michael Molnar in *The Star of Bethlehem: the legacy of the Magi* has shown that there could well have been a real star which led the Magi to Bethlehem.

The Three Holy Kings

by John of Hildesheim

This book in medieval handwriting, was first written in Latin and later printed in German, by Johannes von Hildesheim, c.1370.

This is the beginning of a book, written about the honour, which was offered to our Lord Jesus Christ and his Mother Mary by the Three Holy Kings; it tells how they came to the land of Israel, what they saw there and accomplished, and then how they were parted and separated from each other after death and were brought together again by Helena, and finally how Bishop Reinald brought them to Germany, to Cologne where they rest to this present day.

Chapter 1

Praise, honour and veneration of the Three Holy Kings have been given by Christendom from the rising of the sun to its setting. The Church in the East is honoured by them, for they were the first of heathenism to bring to our Lord Jesus Christ their offerings, and to acknowledge him as God and man; the Church in the West honoured them and still does so with holy love, for their bodies are buried in Cologne. But how they got there, what toils they encountered and trials they endured is not known to everyone. It is for these reasons that this book is written, in honour of our Lord Jesus Christ and his dear Mother Mary.

Chapter 2

First, you must know that Balaam, the Midianite priest who was a heathen prophet, foretold 'There shall come a star out of Jacob and a man shall be born from Israel and he shall have dominion over all the heathen'. Now as Balaam was a heathen, the heathen listened to him and believed his prophecy. Now it is strange that a heathen should have spoken the truth about Christ. But that happened because God wished to be witnessed to by all peoples, even though those who were his enemies had to speak the truth about him. In the same way, he wished to have witness from Caiaphas, the high priest of the Jews, when he said, 'It is better that one man should die than that all the world should perish'. Caiaphas spoke the truth, but did not know it. Balaam foretold it, and was its enemy.

Chapter 3

When the Jews had reached the promised land from Egypt through the Red Sea and had conquered Jerusalem, there was in India a high mountain called VAUS. On this mountain the Indians built a look-out, so as to be warned in case the Jews, the Romans or another nation should invade their country in strength. If the watchers on the mountain should see an army approaching in the distance, they were to kindle a fire so that the country should be warned by the fire at night and by the smoke during the daytime. When Balaam's prophecy was known, the princes of the land took counsel and came to the watchers who guarded the country on their lookout, and gave them money as an incentive to inform them if they should observe a new light or a new star in the heavens. They were then to make it known immediately, for the princes hoped to live to see the time when Balaam's prophecy should be fulfilled – 'There shall rise a star …'

Chapter 4

Later on, about 1200 years after the birth of Christ, there was a famous town called Acre, both large and rich, so much so that many rich princes, lords, citizens and merchants established themselves there, and their reputation reached the end of the world. To this town came the most honourable and mighty from India. They saw that everything was more costly and magnificent than in their own country. They settled there and built a fortress and a royal dwelling, bringing with them much gold and precious stones, including a priceless crown made of gold, pearls and precious stones, and on top of the crown there was a star and in the star a cross. The star was like the one which appeared to the three Kings when they sought our Lord Jesus. This crown, it is said, belonged to King Melchior who offered gold to our Lord. Through God's grace and the merit of the three Kings, it had the virtue of driving out devils, healing the dying and many other illnesses, for those to whom it was shown recovered. This crown with other treasures the Knights Templar preserved in a great treasury and had great benefit from it. But when the Order was dissolved and the Templars expelled, no one, even to this present day, has discovered the whereabouts of the crown and the other precious things, for that reason there was great lamentation everywhere both in town and country.

The aforesaid princes also brought books from India with them to the town of Acre. In them, in the Chaldean language, the life and work of the Holy Three Kings is written and from these and other books, and from the testimony of a believing eyewitness, this book has been compiled.

Chapter 5

Now at the time when those of India were hoping and waiting for the fulfilment of Balaam's prophecy, they consulted together and looked far and wide for twelve stargazers and wise men, offering them rich rewards if they would watch and wait on Mount Vaus, until the star rose so that they might see where he whom the star foretold, and who should reign over all nations, should be born. They also decreed that if one of the twelve should be removed by death, another should immediately take his place. There were many wonders told about Mount Vaus, how high it was and how all around the watch tower were bushes and rare plants, and how on the lookout stood a high stone column with a great golden star on the top which turned with the wind, so that when the sun shone on it by day and the moon by night, it could be seen at a distance in the country round about.

Chapter 6

The time came that God wished to have mercy on mankind and on sinners and that his only-begotten Son should be born of the pure Virgin Mary. It was the time that the Emperor called Octavian ruled; he was so powerful that the whole world was obedient to him. In the forty-second year of his reign, he commanded that all the inhabitants of the whole world should go to their birthplace to pay a tax to the Emperor; its value was a penny and according to the number of pennies received, it would be possible to count the number of people on earth. Joseph lived in Nazareth with our Lady, but he had been born in Bethlehem, the town of David, where his ancestors had settled of old. They wished to obey the Emperor and bring their penny, but when they got near to Bethlehem, it was near the time that Mary should bring forth her child, our Lord. For the same reason many other people had come to

Bethlehem at the same time and all the inns were full. Mary and Joseph came too late to find lodgings, all the more so because people could see that they were poor. So no one paid any attention to them. When Joseph had gone through all the streets, he came at last to a stable built on to a wall which in olden times had been part of the farmhouse of Jesse, the father of David. There was an opening in the wall like a door, which led into a deserted dwelling where no one had gone for many years. On the wall was a little stone crib. Joseph and Mary settled down there and Joseph tied his little donkey to the crib. In front of the stable was a weekly market, where bread, wood, old clothes and all kinds of things were sold, and the people who came in from the villages tied up their donkeys and cattle under the stable roof. Joseph found a child already standing in the stable by the crib. Some writers say the child was Joseph's and he had brought him with him to sell if he were in need, but this book says nothing about that – rather it would suggest that the child belonged to a poor man who could find nowhere to shelter for the night. In this poor, deserted, narrow little shelter the pure Son of God, Jesus Christ, who is the hope of all the world, was born of the pure Virgin Mary. She had nothing to lay the child on, so she laid him in the crib, in front of the donkey and the ox. There was a little hay in the crib, and on this Mary laid the Christ Child wrapped in a cloth, for she had not thought her time was so near. In this humble state was born the Saviour of the world, without pain or suffering.

Chapter 7

All night long there were many shepherds watching their flocks in the fields. An angel of God appeared to them, and a blinding light shone around them, and they were sore afraid. But the angel said: Fear not. I bring you good tidings of great joy. Today is born the Christ, the Saviour of the world, in King David's town. The sign that this is so is that you will find a child laid in a crib and swaddled in a little cloth. Straightway, they heard the clear song of the angels and the heavenly host, singing: *Gloria in excelsis Deo – Glory to God in the highest and peace to men on earth.* Bethlehem, where this occurred, lies two miles from Jerusalem, and of old times was neither great nor renowned, but it is called David's town because David was born there, and right in David's house Christ was born. The place where the shepherds herded their flocks lies half a mile from Bethlehem and is the same place where David grazed his herds and snatched them from the jaws of bears and wolves. The shepherds could spend every night of the year with their flocks in the open at the time Christ was born because there was great peace. In that blessed land, the fields are green at Christmas time and whoever has many flocks buys a meadow and drives them there to graze by day and night. So the shepherds were watching there at that time and the same custom prevails in that country to this day.

Chapter 8

As we have said, while the stargazers were watching all the time for the star to rise, which Balaam had foretold, God performed this miracle and let a star rise as clear as the sun. It stood in the heavens and lighting all lands, it hung like an eagle over the mountains, and remained standing still by night and by day, – not even the sun could banish it. The star had the form of a little child with the sign of the holy cross, and a voice coming out of the star was heard, saying 'Today is born the king of the Jews, he who is awaited by the people, the future Lord'.

Chapter 9

This star was seen throughout India, and everyone was happy, not doubting but that it was the star foretold by

Balaam. India is not one country but is divided into three parts separated from each other by high mountains, making it wearisome and dangerous to travel from one part to another. Each of the three Kings was Lord over one of the three Indias, and when the star shone they were not near to each other, but so far separated that they did not know of each other's existence. When they saw the star and heard the voice which came from it, each of them arose immediately and adorned himself with royal splendour, rich gifts and costly garments and prepared many followers with camels, horses and mules, and hastened to offer prayers in honour of the new King, the new-born Child, not as man but as God. They also prepared beds, domestic needs and food, for they foresaw that they would be a long time on the journey before they found the new-born King.

Chapter 10

The first India was the Kingdom of Nubia, which at the time Christ was born, was ruled over by Melchior who offered gold to our Lord Jesus Christ. Arabia, in which Mount Sinai lay, belonged to Nubia; it is also on the Red Sea, through which it is easy to sail from Syria and Egypt to India. But Christian merchants are not allowed by the Sultan to bring over Christian kings' letters or messages to Prester John, who is lord over India, lest they should ally themselves against him and break his power. Clergy, pilgrims and monks who wish to go to India have to travel by a really long and irksome way through the kingdom of Persia. Natives who are allowed to sail all over the Red Sea from one land to another say its depths are so red that it looks like red wine, though the water itself is like any other, but salty, yet it is so pure and clear that you can see stones and fishes on the bottom. It is at least four miles wide, and the Jews passed over it dryshod when King Pharaoh pursued them wishing to slay them. Out of the

The Adoration of the Magi from the Franciscan Friary, Dundee.

The Adoration of the Magi, St Gregory's church, Kirknewton, Northumberland. The origin is unknown and the dating uncertain, but probably pre-9th century.

A stone sculpture of the Three Kings, originally from Thetford Priory in Norfolk and now found in S: Peter Hungate museum in Norwich.

An alabaster of the Adoration of the Magi, 1350, at Long Melford, Suffolk.

A reredos of the Three Kings, presented to the parish church of St Nicholas, Aberdeen, by King Robert III (1390–1406), now in the chapel of the Blessed Virgin.

Our Lady and the Three Kings, St Mary's church, Haddington.

The Three Kings Shrine, Cologne Cathedral.

Foster's Almshouse chapel, Colston Street, Bristol. Built by John Foster, merchant, and dedicated to the Three Kings of Cologne in 1484.

Red Sea rises a river called the Nile which flows through Egypt to Babylon and Alexandria. Rich merchandise is brought to the West from India on this river. In Arabia all the soil is red and the stone and wood produced on the land is all red, as is the gold mined there. There is a vein of emerald on Mount Sinai, but the Sultan's servants guard it well. The land formerly belonged to Prester John, but now mostly to the Sultan, though it still owes tribute to Prester John.

Chapter 11

The second India is called Godolia, ruled over at that time by King Balthazar, who offered incense to our Lord. In this kingdom is a land called Saba, where many plants grow, more than in other lands, and especially there is found the best incense, which runs out of trees.

Chapter 12

In the third India is the kingdom of Tharsis, which at that time was ruled over by King Caspar, who offered incense[1] to our Lord. The famous island Eyrisoulla lies in this land: it is there that the holy apostle St Thomas is buried. Myrrh grows more plentifully on this island than in other lands. It grows in the shape of burnt spikes and when it is ripe, it is soft, and anyone going through the field finds it hanging on his clothes. Ropes and cords are pulled through the plants to gather it, for it hangs on to these and it can then be stripped off like soft wax. Although the three Kings had large territories, yet God wanted the parts from which these offerings that were brought to our Lord came, to be specified. So the prophet in the Psalter speaks of Kings of Tharsis and of the isles who offered, and Kings of Arabia

[1]Obviously a misprint for myrrh.

and Saba who brought gifts. That is why silence is observed about the great kingdoms they possessed and they are only known by these small districts.

Chapter 13

How the Three Holy Kings prepared themselves with great joy, as described above, and what each of them brought from his own district, none of the others knew, and the star went before all three, in front of one just as before the others. When they stopped, so did the star. In the night, it did not shine as the moon but as the sun, and because there was peace in all the world at that time, every town remained open all night. If it was broad daylight, the people ran into the fields and gazed at the foot marks and hoof marks, asking each other what it all meant. If there were many bogs or moors in the land so that it was difficult to cross from one country to another, Almighty God so arranged that all these things did not lead them astray and the roads were dry and traversable. The Kings did not rest nor sleep, they neither ate nor drank, they went into no hostelry, nor did their attendants, their cows, mules or horses, until they had reached Bethlehem and fulfilled their offering, their service and their prayer. It was there that they first ate and drank and slept, as it is written later. Nevertheless, it all seemed but one day and by divine strength the star led them to their goal in thirteen days. One early morning at sunrise, they all came and found Mary, still in the poor little house and Jesus still in the crib. If anyone should think this impossible, they should read in the prophet Daniel how the angel of God took the prophet Habbakuk from the land of Judaea, when he should have taken food to the reapers in the field, and carried him in an hour to Babylon to Daniel who lay in prison, and gave him the food to eat which the reapers should have had, and then took Habbakuk again by the hair and brought him back to the place where he had found him. That took place in a short hour, and the distance between Judaea and Babylon is more than a hundred miles by water and land. Almighty God who did such a thing in the Old Testament could in the New Testament easily bring the Three Kings from India to Judaea in thirteen days.

Chapter 14

As the Three Kings made their way separately until they were about two miles from Jerusalem, there came down a very thick fog which enveloped them and obscured all the land round about, and in the fog they lost the star. It came to pass that King Melchior came to Mount Calvary where afterwards our Lord Jesus Christ was martyred and the two thieves received their punishment. King Melchior stopped there with his companions and went no further for the fog grew thicker and thicker. At the same time, King Bathazar from Saba and Godolia with his retinue, approaching by another way, camped on the Mount of Olives by the little village Galilee which is often mentioned in the Gospel because there our Lord appeared to his disciples after his death. But another Galilee is mentioned, and that is a country three days journey from Jerusalem. As the two Kings stayed in the mountains, the fog lifted, but the star did not shine. When the fog vanished, they both went no further, nor did they recognise each other. Meanwhile King Caspar of Tharsis arrived with his people by a third road, and lighted upon Mount Calvary, and as the fog had completely gone, the three Lords went together almost to Jerusalem. One of the retinue began to talk with those of the others and asked what they were looking for. When they discovered that all three had come for the same reason, they were very happy and rode together; they embraced and kissed each other and were more zealous and eager in their search than before. So they rode all together towards Jerusalem.

As they drew near to the city, they were full of joy and hoped to find the new King in the capital. The number of their attendants was so great that some had to be left outside the city, and assembled there, so that it looked as if Jerusalem was being besieged. Herod and all Jerusalem were troubled at this, and when they asked where the king of the country was, they were still more worried for they were afraid of war and the destruction of their country. The Gospel puts this quite clearly: 'When Jesus was born in Bethlehem in the days of Herod the king, there came kings from the east to Jerusalem, and asked where the king of the country was. Then was King Herod sore troubled and all Jerusalem with him. The Kings said, "We have seen his star in the East and are come with gifts to worship him".' King Herod sent into the town for the elders and wisest men and asked them where Christ should be born, and they answered 'In Bethlehem in Judaea, for thus saith the Prophet, And thou Bethlehem in the land of Judah art not the least among the princes of Judah; for out of thee shall came a ruler who will govern my people Israel.' Then Herod summoned the Kings secretly and ascertained from them what time the star appeared and sent them to Bethlehem. And the star which they had seen in the East again went before them until it came to the place where the Child lay, and there it stayed still in the air.

Chapter 15

When the Three Holy Kings had heard from the Jews where the King should be born, they set off with their attendants to Bethlehem, and the star again went before them. They came to the place where the angel on Christmas Eve had appeared to the shepherds, and they found the shepherds who told them how the angel of God had spoken to them at that time, of the light which had shone upon them, and how they had seen the Child. The Lords listened to them with joy and took particular notice of their words and also richly rewarded them, and then rode on happily to Bethlehem. There they paused and laid aside their stately robes and prepared to see the King. When they went down the street at the end of which the lowly hut lay, the star remained stationary there and went no further, but sank down with such brilliant rays that the whole hut and everything in it was lighted up. Then it went back on high, and remained motionless while its light still streamed down into the hut.

Chapter 16

On the day that the Three Kings brought the child their offering, Jesus was thirteen days old and lay in the crib wound round with mean clothes. Mary his Mother was comely in form, with a dusky complexion, and she wore a poor blue cloak. But the Three Kings were gloriously apparelled. Melchior, the King of Nubia and Arabia, who offered gold, was the smallest of stature. Balthazar, the King of Saba, who offered incense, was of medium stature, and Caspar, the King of Tharsis, who brought myrrh, was the tallest and a Moor. This is not extraordinary for the prophet foretold it in the psalm: Ethiopians shall kneel before him (Ps. 72). It should also be noted that the nearer people live to the sun rising, the smaller they are, but plants, worms and animals are much more lively and stronger than in this country; the same applies to birds, whether wild or tame.

Chapter 17

It is known that the Three Kings brought much treasure and many costly clothes with them from their own countries, for all the jewels which Alexander the Great had left behind at his death, the gifts which the Queen of Sheba had received from King Solomon and all which he left to give honour to God, had come into the possession of the Three Kings. Their ancestors had destroyed the Temple at Jerusalem, and now the Three Kings brought all this treasure with them to honour the new King. But when they came to the mean little hut where Jesus lay, there was such an indescribable clarity that they stood as in a glow and were unable to think where they were for astonishment. So they quickly felt in their sacks and offered whatever came first into their hands, and forgot the good things they had brought with them. Melchior offered thirty golden pennies and a golden apple which came into his hand; Balthazar offered incense, and Caspar myrrh, and they completely forgot what Mary said to them, remembering nothing except that she humbly bowed to each King, and said 'Thanks be to God'. The golden apple which Melchior offered with the thirty golden pennies had belonged to Alexander the Great, and he had had it made so pliable that it could be gripped in the hand. For Alexander had conquered the whole world and held it in his hand, and for this reason he had had the apple made as a symbol, because the world is round, and the symbol means that he was as powerful over the whole world as over the apple. And as the apple was given to the child in the hand, that was a sign that all earthly power is vain before God and will crumble into dust and ashes.

Chapter 18

When the Lords had fulfilled their offering so nobly, food was prepared for them and their followers, and after they had eaten, they and their servants lay down and slept a day and a night. God's angel appeared to them in their sleep and warned them not to go back to Herod. They all decided to do this and to return home to their own countries another way, and it took them two years before they reached home. On the way, they had to stay at inns, eat, drink and sleep in an ordinary human way, for the star shone for them no longer. Wherever they stayed for a night's rest, they told the people of the country everything that had happened to them. Their return was thus known and publicised in all the countries so that it could never be forgotten or wiped out, although it was against King Herod and the Jews. Although they were on the way home for two years, no one gave them anything for their needs, for they had brought great provision with them from home, and they all came safe and sound to Vaus, where the star had first shone.

Chapter 19

Now when Herod learnt that the Kings had gone home, he was very angry, prepared a strong force and went after them. Wherever they went, the country folk spoke of the Kings and their attendants and how rich they were, and this grieved Herod and his people. He came to a town from which the Kings had sailed over the water and there Herod avenged himself on the inhabitants, burnt their ships and laid waste their land. When Herod and his attendants returned home and heard the true tale of how the heathen had made their journey in thirteen days, contrary to the natural run of things, he could not wonder enough, and was more angry than before. The Jews said that the Three Kings were sorcerers and had accomplished the journey by means of black art: others called them astrologers, because it had been brought about through the star, and so the custom grew up to call them Magi, which means both sorcerers and astrologers.

Chapter 20

When the Lords reached Vaus after their two years' journey, they settled down with their people and built a beautiful chapel on the peak of the mountain to the glory and honour of the young King whom they had sought and found. They rested in the town of Stulls which lay at the foot of the mountain after their difficult journey, and chose a common burying place for when they should die, so that all three should lie by one another. They vowed to come there every year with a large following, and when that occurred, they were received with great pomp by the highest nobles of the country who rode out to meet them, praising God for working such a great wonder through them. The Kings also preached about it in every land they passed through, and this was the reason why many heathen set up a star in their temples, in which there was a picture of a child. Every year they went to the chapel on Mount Vaus, bringing their offerings. The Three Kings likewise set up the star containing the figure of a child in their own countries and renounced the world more and more, humbly living godly lives until the time of the Ascension of Christ into heaven.

Chapter 21

After the Three Kings had brought their offerings to our Lord in Bethlehem, the news of the birth of the Child, of the visit of the Three Kings and the shepherds spread abroad, and Herod and the Jews were greatly annoyed. Mary and Joseph were right in the midst of it, and they arose and left their wretched hut and went to another poor one. They stayed there until Mary had taken the Child to the Temple, and were loved by man and woman alike, and together with all their belongings were taken care of and well hidden, so that the powers that be could not find them. However, in the hurry and fear in which Mary left their first hut, she forgot the little cloth in which the Child had first been wrapped, as well as her chemise. So they remained lying in the crib and in the hay till the time when the honoured lady Helena, mother of the Emperor Constantine, came there and found them as fresh and whole as the first day, for the Jews, through their hate, had so discredited the hut in which Christ was born, and forbidden anyone to go into it, and so it stood for more than two hundred years, desolate and ruined. But the chemise and swaddling clothes Helena found undamaged, for it is quite to be expected that the worthiness of the pure body in which it was wrapped should prevent it from rotting. On the spot where our Lady last stayed until she presented the Child in the Temple, the honourable Lady Helena afterwards built a beautiful chapel to the honour of the Three Kings and St Nicholas, as the Christian faith grew and spread abroad. Through this chapel, a public street ran for a long time, for there were two doors, of which one is now filled up. The stone on which our Lady sat and suckled her child can still be seen, and one day by accident her breast slipped from the Child, and a drop of milk fell on the stone. The colour of the milk can still be seen today on the very spot and no one can remove it.

Chapter 22

Now the time had come that the Child should be carried to church on the fortieth day after his birth, so Mary and Joseph took him to Jerusalem and offered the sacrifice in obedience to the Law of Moses. The old prophet Simeon took the Child in his arms, and said the *Nunc dimittis servum tuum Domine*. Old Simeon had been blind for many years but at that moment he could see again. There was also an old widow, Anna, who prophesied much blessedness for the Child at the same time. When the prophecies of Simeon and Anna were pronounced, some of the oldest and wisest of the Jews were present, and so it got back to Herod. Then Mary and her Child were no longer in safety, and one night the Angel of the Lord appeared to St Joseph, and said, 'Arise and take the Child and his Mother and flee into Egypt and stay there until I give you word again; for

Herod will seek the Child to kill him'. Joseph arose in the night and took the Child and his beloved Mother and fled to Egypt. So Mary left the country by night, and how she went on her way is described in a little book called *Our Lord's Childhood*.

Chapter 23

It is twelve days' journey from Jerusalem to the place in Egypt where Mary lay hid, and on the road she took from Bethlehem to Egypt and back again roses still grow, called Roses of Jericho, and they are found nowhere else. Saracen women are fond of using these roses when in childbirth. The shepherds who watch their flocks in their fields by night break off roses and give them to pilgrims and merchants, and so they travel far and wide over the world and bring back the memory of the Flight into Egypt.

Chapter 24

Mary stayed there for seven years and lived near the town of New Babylon and Cairo where the Sultan's house is today. These towns lie very close to each other and are seven times as large as Paris. In the town where Mary lived there is now a balsam herb garden. The garden is not big, but it contains seven springs in which Mary washed the Child's swaddling clothes. The balsam grows on stalks no higher than an ell, the shrubs are like rose bushes and the leaves like clover. Every bush has its guardian who has to be a Christian, and must keep it clean and watered with as much care as he has for his own body. In March, the Sultan himself comes and attends to the garden, and cuts back the wood in the same way as vines are pruned. The cuttings are tied up in silk and a little silver bottle is hung from them, into which the balsam drips through the silk. When it has stopped dripping, the Sultan takes the balsam and keeps it, and when kings and noblemen send to him for balsam, he gives them a little glass a finger high. But when the Sultan has gone away, the guardians take the prunings of the bushes by his orders and simmer them in a clean dish, and what comes out of the wood rises to the top like oil. This is thick and looks like young must. When anyone is bruised or falls down or is hurt in other ways, this balsam is placed on the spot, and every wound which is anointed with it is healed and disappears immediately. Herdsmen sell the balsam from this bush to pilgrims, and they spread it over the world. But it cannot be compared with what drips first from the bushes themselves, for if anyone should allow a little drop to fall on his hand, it goes right through and out the other side, and the place through which it passed never heals again. This balsam is raw, while the other is described as boiled. It is the belief of everyone in the East that this balsam came into being so that Mary could wash her Child's clothes in the garden and hang them on the bushes to dry, and this is proved by the fact that only Christians may tend the garden, and when any other people have been commanded to tend the garden, the bushes have dried up and rotted, but as soon as Christians came back, they sprang to life again.

Chapter 25

Curious things are written about the thirty florins which King Melchior offered our Lord. The coins were of gold and Ninis, a king of Mesopotamia had them cast, and the man who cast them was Than, Abraham's father. Part of them came to Abraham, but how is not known. When Abraham left his home at God's command, he took the coins with him to Hebron, and with them bought a field for a burial place for himself, his wife Sara and their children. With the same coins, King Pharaoh's courtier Potiphar, bought Joseph, Jacob's son, from Joseph's brothers who were also Jacob's sons. The brothers brought the same coins to Egypt to buy corn. But when Jacob, the father of the twelve brothers died, Joseph sent to Sheba to buy spices to anoint his father's body for burial. Later the Queen of Sheba took the thirty coins with other costly jewels and presented them to King Solomon. When Solomon died and Jerusalem was destroyed, they went to the King of Arabia as booty. He was an ally of the King of Egypt, but he put them in the royal treasury. King Melchior was an heir of this King of Arabia, and so they passed from one person to another until finally King Melchior offered them to our Lord Jesus, as we have written above.

Chapter 26

When Mary and her Child had to flee to Egypt, she tied up the coins with the incense and myrrh in a cloth, and left it in the wilderness. A herdsman, who fed his cattle in the wilderness, found the treasure, and took charge of it until our Lord preached and worked signs in Judaea. Now it happened that this herdsman fell ill, and did not know how to cure this illness. He heard that there was a man in Judaea who healed the sick without medicine. The herdsman arose and remembered his treasure which he had found a long time before, so he took it with him and went to Judaea and found our Lord Jesus Christ. He begged him of his mercy to help him. Our Lord Jesus Christ who never refused a request, helped the poor man and restored his health. When he felt that he had been healed, he took the thirty pennies with the incense and myrrh and offered it to our Lord as a thanksgiving for his goodness. Our Lord Jesus knew well where the treasure was from, and told the herdsman to offer what he had in his hands at the altar in the Temple. The priest who officiated at the altar took the thirty pennies and cast them into the box; the incense he burnt as required and the myrrh he put aside. A bitter drink was made from this myrrh which was offered to Christ to drink when he hung on the cross and said 'I thirst'. The rest of the myrrh Nicodemus took and used it at the burial of Jesus. But the thirty pennies were given to Judas that he might betray Jesus. When he repented of his betrayal, he threw them down at the feet of the Jews and went and hanged himself. The pennies were picked up and half were given to the soldiers who watched over the grave of Jesus; a field for the burial of poor pilgrims was bought with the other fifteen. This field lay near Jerusalem and is no longer nor wider than a stone's throw. No one should think it strange that these pennies are described in the gospel as silver pieces, for actually they were made of the purest Arabian gold: Holy Writ calls all money silver pieces. These pennies were never separated until cut. Each of these pennies was worth three florins in value and weight and on one side appears a King's head crowned with laurel and on the other Chaldaean letters which no one can read.

Chapter 27

When our Lady had been seven years in Egypt and Herod was dead, the angel said to Joseph, 'Get up and take the Child and his mother and go from Egypt back to the land of Judaea, for they are dead who sought the young child's life'. Joseph did as the angel commanded, and returned to Judaea. But when he heard that Herod's son was ruling in his father's place, he was afraid to go to Jerusalem and went to a little town called Nazareth. There Jesus was brought up by his mother and all that happened until he ascended into heaven is told by the Evangelists.

Chapter 28

When the twelve holy apostles were sent out by Christ to preach in all the world, St Thomas had to go to India, although it was a hard task. The Indians at that time had received very good teaching. The Three Holy Kings who had seen our Lord as a child, preached, and announced his birth in all countries and towns. The apostles Bartholomew, Simon and Jude were also sent there. No one should wonder that all these apostles were sent to preach the gospel, for as we said above, the Indies are three, one larger and wider than the other and the smallest larger than the whole of the country on this side of the Mediterranean. So St Thomas came to the land of the Three Kings, and preached the holy Christian faith, healed the sick, raised the dead, cast out devils, converted the heathen and pulled down pagan temples. Now it happened that in one heathen church he saw a stone erected with a star upon it; in the star was the figure of a child and over it a cross was carved, just as the Holy Kings had seen it, and they had set up copies throughout the whole of heathendom. St Thomas asked the heathen priests what sort of sign it was and what it meant. The heathen priests told him of the Three Kings and everything that had happened from beginning to end, how the star had shone for them on Mount Vaus, and how in thirteen days they had travelled to Bethlehem and found the Child, and how it took them two years to return home. They told everything they had heard about the Three Holy Kings. When St Thomas heard this he was filled with great joy, and from that time was more fervent in preaching than before. He told the priests about our Lord's conception, birth, childhood, life, sufferings, death, resurrection and ascension, and how he himself had heard our Lord's words from his own mouth. He interpreted the gifts of the Three Kings in a spiritual sense, and he consecrated all the temples of the heathen which had been built for the devil, to the honour of the Child whom their Kings had sought and worshipped. So the fame of St Thomas, his teaching and the great wonders he worked by divine power resounded far and wide throughout the country, until it reached the Three Kings.

Chapter 29

When St Thomas heard of the Three Kings and they of him, he wished with all his heart to find them alive. Similarly, they also wished to see St Thomas so that he might tell them how it stood with the Child whom they had gone so far to seek. So it was that each of the Three Kings in his own country prepared to see St Thomas, and although they were now old and frail, yet they set out with a great following of nobles and gentlemen, met St Thomas and received him with great reverence while he received them with great happiness and humility. He preached to them and told them all that had happened to our Lord Christ from the beginning to the end, and he baptised them with all their people. So they were filled with the grace of the Holy Ghost, and helped St Thomas to proclaim God's Word; they preached the Christian faith as ardently and worthily as St Thomas himself. What they preached St Thomas illustrated from Holy Writ and the prophets and what Thomas told of the Lord's life and resurrection and sufferings, they confirmed and supported by telling of his holy childhood which they had seen with their own eyes.

Then the Three Holy Kings with St Thomas and all the people went to Mount Vaus and, to the great joy of the people, St Thomas consecrated the chapel which stood on the mountain to the honour of our Lord Jesus Christ. From then onwards, people made pilgrimages from far and near to Mount Vaus, and their number increased from year to year so that the town which lay under the mountain grew to such an extent that there is now no more famous town to be found in the whole of India. This town was the dwelling of Prester John, who is Lord of India, while St Thomas is the Patriarch of India.

Chapter 30

When St Thomas had converted all the people to God and baptised the Three Kings, he then ordained them priest. For they had no wives, and tradition maintains that all three were virgins and remained so until their death. They were also the first of heathendom to adopt the faith and to sacrifice to the true God. St Thomas also consecrated bishops and priests in all their countries and taught them how to celebrate Mass, baptise and teach the Paternoster and Credo. With the help of the Three Kings he also gave the priests land and other property, consecrated pagan temples as Christian churches, pulled down the altars of idols and performed many wonders through faith in our Lord Christ. It was for all this that he received the martyr's crown: in the country where he was martyred the people had heads like dogs, only not rough or hard – in India there are many extraordinary people.

Chapter 31

After the death of St Thomas, the Three Holy Kings sent deputies to all the priests and bishops whom St Thomas had ordained, and also to all the nobles and gentlemen in their lands, and summoned them with their consent to a council, so that they might choose a worthy man as his successor, who would be their Lord and Father in holy things. This man should be called Thomas after the holy Apostle, and when he died, another should be chosen with the same name, and this custom should continue until the end of the world. Now there was a worthy man with the name of James Antiochus, who had followed St Thomas into the land of India. He was unanimously chosen and put in the place of St Thomas as patriarch, changing his name to Thomas, as still today the patriarchs of India are called. The people of India obey Thomas in holy things as we here in this country obey the Pope of Rome.

Chapter 32

When all this had been done, the Three Holy Kings, who had no children nor heirs, took counsel with their nobles and gentlemen, and chose from their number a noble and steadfast man, who after their death should be lord in temporal things in their lands and kingdoms for ever. If anyone tried to practise malice or wrong on bishops or priests, or disturb or put down the Christian faith which had been newly adopted, this man should go to war and take over their lands. This protector of spiritual matters should not be called king or emperor for the sake of humility, but should be known as Prester John. For there is nothing more worthy under the sun than priests, for God has given them the power to bind and loose, and to consecrate his holy Body and lift it up. Christ never commissioned his Mother or any angel into this Order, and kings and emperors bow before them. He was called John, for John the apostle was our Lord's beloved disciple, and was also a priest, and John the Baptist baptised our Lord, and of those born of women there was none greater than John the Baptist. So it was for all the worthiness of this name that he should be called Prester John, and for the same reason live in virtue, holiness and honour and the people should be obedient to him in all worldly things.

Chapter 33

As the Three Kings had now properly arranged everything and cared for their country and people, they remained together in the town Stulla, which was situated at the foot of Mount Vaus, but only lived there for another two years. One fine day, not long after Christmas, a beautiful star shone over the town, which had never been seen before.

The Three Kings knew well that their end was drawing near, and that God wished to raise them up into eternal life, so they had a beautiful tomb made which would be worthy of them. When they had devoutly and commendably begun to keep the feast of Christmas, King Melchior died on the eighth day, after saying Mass. He was 116 years old. The two other Kings took up his body and buried him in the ground with great honour. Then on the fifteenth day, nearly on the feast of the Epiphany of the Lord, Balthazar, King of Saba, died after saying Mass. He was 112 years old. He was buried by the last King in the same tomb next to Melchior. Seven days afterwards, Caspar the third King died after celebrating Mass. He was 109 years old, and he too was buried with great honour by the people, and as he was lowered into the tomb, the other two moved away from one another and allowed their companion to lie between them. Everyone present perceived that as the Lords had loved each other in life, so in death they should not be parted. The star which had shone before their death remained motionless over the place until their bodies were translated as will be described later.

Chapter 34

When the Three Holy Kings had gone to God away from this land of exile, God, who had loved them here below, but still more in eternal life, honoured them after their death. For old and young, men and women, suffering from any kind of sickness, wherever they dwelt, either near or far, on water or land, were helped by God when they called upon the Three Kings, to honour them. So it came about that people from every land visited their tomb, and the signs and wonders which were wrought after their death confirmed the Christian faith they had learned in life. Their bodies and the priestly vestments in which they had been buried remained as fresh as if they were still alive and only slept, not as if they were dead.

Chapter 35

After this, during a long period, the wicked spirit sowed his seeds among the people of India, so that they abandoned the Christian faith and were divided amongst themselves so that many schisms and heresies arose. Resorting to the tomb of the Three Kings decreased, and the town of Stulla declined. The Three Kings' bodies grew pale and ashen grey like other dead bodies and their priestly vestments rotted and went to dust. The nobles and lords of the family of the Three Kings who remained in the town of Stulla also dissented from each other in the faith. Each family took their own king back to their own land; they were buried with great honour in the most famous town of their land. So for a long time they were separated.

Chapter 36

But when the time came that Almighty God wished to separate the bad from the good, as the tares from the wheat, counting some 300 years from the time of God's birth when the powerful Emperor Constantine was healed through baptism of his unclean leprosy after being converted from heathenism to the Christian faith by Pope St Sylvester – and this baptism greatly strengthened the Christian Faith – there lived the honoured lady, Helena, the Emperor's mother, in the land of Judaea across the sea. She held much with the Jewish faith and little with the Christian. She was not pleased that the Emperor had become a Christian, and she wrote him a letter in which she scolded him. The son wrote back and justified himself, and God caused the honourable Helena to become a Christian herself. So it was that she who before had praised the Jews now began to reprove them and to look for the places where our Lord Jesus had been, the place where he was born and where he suffered the passion, and those places which formerly she had hated as much as the Jews, she now began to honour with the Christians. She began to enquire eagerly about the Cross and the nails of our Lord Jesus Christ, and compelled the Jews to tell her, and when she found it and the nails she built a beautiful great church over the places where Christ had suffered death, where he was buried and where he appeared to Mary Magdalene. This church enclosed all these places under one roof. She did the same in other places where our Lord had been, and built churches, convents and chapels, giving them a sufficient endowment, and furnishing them with monks, parish priests and bishops. In the town where the angel appeared to the shepherds, as told above, she built a beautiful church, called 'Gloria in excelsis', and as the Seven Hours begin with *Deus in adjutorium meum intende*, so to this day in that place, they begin with *Gloria in excelsis.*

Chapter 37

When these things had been done, the worthy Helena came to Bethlehem to the little hut in which our dear Lord was born. It had long been shut up, and was so dilapidated that neither man nor beast had dared to enter it. She came to the crib in which he who was at the same time God and Man had been laid, and found the hay and the napkins, and also our Lady's chemise which she had forgotten when she had fled from the hut in fear. Helena took that with her to Constantinople, and everything was still as fresh and in exactly the same condition as at first. She preserved it all with great honour in the church of St Sophia, and it remained there until the time that King Charlemagne came to Greece and helped the Christians there to regain their lands and towns. They gave him the chemise and napkins, and this great Christian King brought them with him to Aachen where they are still to this day displayed in our Lady's Minster, which Charlemagne himself founded.

Chapter 38

The worthy Lady Helena also built a splendid Minster on the spot where Christ was born, only it is not vaulted but instead roofed with timber and lead. From the choir, you can go straight into a mean underground place which is where Christ our Lord and God was born, and by the altar stands the stone crib in which Christ lay in front of the ox and the ass, and where the Three Kings worshipped him. In this crypt St Jerome also lived and the noble Roman widow Paula with her daughter Eustasia, and they are buried there. In the church seventy marble pillars stand holding up the building and it is decorated with jewels within and without. Helena not only erected the church but also provided an archbishop and cathedral canons, who sing the *Gloria in excelsis* in all Masses, even at requiems. The Jews out of hate call the worthy Helena a stable woman because she founded such a splendid church over the stable where Christ was born. For this reason a tablet is exhibited on Christmas night on which St Jerome, who lies buried in the church, had written with his own hand 'The worthy Helena is a good stable woman, for she sought for the crib of our Lord so zealously, and decorated it.' On the spot where the Three Holy Kings knelt in worship of the Child Jesus, there stands a large golden star on the feast of the Epiphany of the Lord and on the feast of the Three Holy Kings, and it is pulled with cords from one end of the church to the other in memory of the way in which the star led the Three Holy Kings and showed them the way.

Chapter 39

When the worthy Lady Helena had finished the church, she went to Nazareth where Christ was brought up. This town lies very pleasantly in a valley of green meadows, and is not walled because the houses are scattered. In the town the worthy Helena built a delightful church. In it is enclosed the room in which our dear Lady was in prayer when Gabriel announced the tidings that she should bear God's Son. In the room, there stands a pillar by which the angel stood when he spoke to the maid and knelt before her. The angel's picture is printed on the pillar like a seal of wax. In the evening when the sun goes to rest and shines on the picture, it is the time that Gabriel announced the tidings to our Lady. When Christians possessed the Holy Land, servants were appointed to ring a bell hanging on the pillar when the sun touched the picture, and whoever heard the sound knelt down and said three Ave Marias: it was from this that the custom of saying Ave Marias in honour of the Virgin in the evening arose. In front of the door of the room is a gushing spring from which the Virgin often drew water, and by this spring the angel spoke to her and comforted her. Pilgrims fill their bottles at this spring and take them home with them, and lame and frail people are healed by it. The Saracens wanted to destroy the spring, but every time they destroyed it, the stronger it sprang up again and flowed. Not far from Nazareth is a lofty mountain called Tabor, and thither went our Lord and the apostles, Peter, James and John, when he showed them his divine Transfiguration. On the mountain the worthy Helena built a beautiful monastery with walls and towers like a castle, and it is inhabited by monks of the Order of St Benedict. On St Sixtus' day, they celebrate the Transfiguration with new wine; all the churches of the Orient celebrate this day as their dedication feast, and put up flags and decorate themselves with many ornaments. Mount Tabor lies four days' journey from Jerusalem, and our Lord journeyed between the two, teaching his disciples, preaching and healing on the way.

Chapter 40

When the worthy Empress Helena had completed all these things, had built so many beautiful churches and staffed them with priests and bishops, and had also discovered the Holy Cross, she began to think seriously about the Three Holy Kings and travelled all over the countries, as all the world at that time was under Roman rule. She came with a great following to India, where she found that the people had departed from the faith which St Thomas and the Three Holy Kings had taught them. She threw down the heathen idols and restored signs of the Holy Spirit by founding monasteries, bishoprics and parishes, and very greatly strengthened Christians in all lands. The people were very happy about this, and the lords of the countries came to the lady and rejoiced with her that she had found the Holy Cross and furnished all the places where our Lord had been with costly buildings. This was very distasteful to the heathen and to some of the Jews. However she was given a general idea where the Three Kings lay buried, and was told how they had lived and died and about all the things this little book has narrated so far. Then the worthy Helena became more earnest and zealous than before, so that God seeing her desire bestowed his grace and enabled her to find the Three Holy Kings. As all lands were under Roman rule, she was granted by the nobles of the countries and especially Prester John, that the bodies of two of the Kings, Melchior and Balthazar should be handed over to her to honour her and to show their love from her son, Constantine, who was Emperor of Rome. But the third King, Caspar, had been carried to the island Egrysculla by the Nestorians, a heretical body, who kept it in a strong, well guarded castle on the island so that no one could capture it by force or prayer, for they said they would rather die than allow their lord to be taken from them.

Chapter 41

The worthy Helena could not bear the Three Kings to be separated, so she sent noble princes and lords to the rulers of the land to obtain the third King for her. In the end she suggested that she should obtain the body of St Thomas the Apostle, and give it to the Nestorians in exchange for that of King Caspar so that she could bring all the Three Kings together. The body of St Thomas had already twice been in the possession of the Nestorians, so it seemed right to give it them again in order to fulfil such a proper purpose. It is a common saying on that island and in the country that one day, the body of St Thomas will be taken from them and brought to Cologne, where he would rest by the Three Holy Kings until the last day.

Chapter 42

When the worthy Helena had brought the third King to the other two all the surroundings were filled with an indescribably noble scent beyond the wonder of man. Then the noble Empress Helena, the mother of the Emperor, took the Three Kings and brought them to the most splendid capital of Greece, called Constantinople, because the Emperor Constantine had built it. When she arrived there with the Three Holy Kings, she was given a wonderful and honourable reception by everyone. A beautiful minster, called St Sophia, stood in the town, so high and broad that it is larger than any in the world, so that the largest ship that sails on the sea, might go into it with all its sails and masts, and move round and round. In the church are many marble pillars which the Emperor alone with a little child and the help of God had set up. Our Lord's seamless robe is also in the church, and the three nails with which Christ was nailed to the Cross, and many other valuable relics to which the Greeks did not attach much value. The thorn crown with which Christ was crowned was there also: it is now in Paris in the chapel of the Kings of France. It occurred at one time that the Emperor was suffering much trouble and damage from the Tartars and Saracens, and he asked holy Louis, King of France, to come to his help. King Louis gave him so much help that he regained his land and people, and in exchange for his help, the Emperor gave King Louis the crown. The next day it was taken to St Laurence's in Paris, and the French were very pleased, but it made the Greeks sad, and they still hope that one day the crown will come back into their possession. In the minster of St Sophia in Constantinople there is a little marble pillar with a statue of the Emperor on a brazen horse well gilded, and next to the pillar the worthy Helena buried the Three Kings with great pomp and ceremony. Streams of people from far and near came to the place, and many wonders and signs were wrought, not only upon those who came but also on those who invoked the Kings at home. This continued for many years. But when Constantine and his worthy mother had died, weeds grew up again and heathendom flourished, so that Christians were persecuted and martyred. There was an Emperor called Julian, who was a Christian, but when he came to power, he forsook the faith, and treated Christians worse than if he had never been a Christian himself. During this period, the Three Holy Kings remained without honour and no one paid any attention to them. The Saracens and Turks got the upper hand and menaced Greece.

Chapter 43

At that time there was a Roman Emperor called Mauritius, who helped the people of Constantinople with assistance from Milan. A writing had been discovered telling how the Emperor sent a learned man called Eustorgius, with an embassy to Milan. He was a wise man, born in Greece, and became confidential and powerful for the Emperor. The people of Milan chose this Eustorgius as their bishop. The Emperor gave him the Three Kings as a reward for his wise counsel and useful service. So the afore-mentioned Bishop Eustorgius brought the Three Kings to Milan and placed them in a church where God also worked many wonders and signs for their sake.

Chapter 44

Now in the year which we reckon as 1163, the people of Milan rose up against the Emperor Frederick Barbarossa. The Emperor took counsel and ranged himself with many proud knights before the town of Milan, and said he would destroy the town. Then the chief nobles of the town took the bodies of the Three Kings and hid them in a secret place. Now there was a bishop of Cologne, called Reinald, who was the Emperor's trusted servant. God brought it about that the town was taken. The Bishop of Cologne placed himself before the palace which belonged to a lord whom the Emperor hated above all others. The Bishop took the palace and went inside. The lord of the Palace came secretly to the Bishop and begged him to make atonement for him to the Emperor if he could, and restore him to favour again. In return for this he would help him to get hold of the Three Kings. The Bishop promised to do this, and held him to it, and brought the lord into the Emperor's favour again. Then the lord showed the Bishop of Cologne where the Three Kings lay. With his faithful servants he took up the Kings and begged the Emperor to give him the Three Kings. The Emperor granted his request and gave them to him. When the Bishop returned home, he placed the Three Kings with great honour in his cathedral. There they lie to this day, together, for as they had loved each other in this life, God did not wish that they should be separated, neither in life nor in death. The Cathedral in which Bishop Philip of Weinsberg, Bishop Reinald's successor, buried the bones of the Three Holy Kings was actually the old one built in the time of Charlemagne and Bishop Hildebold, which was burnt down in the middle of the thirteenth century. The people of Cologne were overjoyed at the arrival of the Three Holy Kings, and from that time looked upon them as the treasure of their town, and placed three crowns in their coat of arms. Almighty God also worked many signs and wonders for their sake from that time to the present day, and pilgrimages were made to them from distant lands by princes, nobles and other folk. Great offerings were made, so great that they could not be measured. Huge presents came from all countries so that the Church of Cologne was enriched for ever. When the old cathedral was burnt, Bishop Conrad imagined that his treasure would be inexhaustible, and began building the new cathedral in which the Three Holy Kings now rest, and shall rest till the Last Day. And with this, the cathedral will be completed with new zeal after six hundred years.

Chapter 45

In the land of India and throughout the whole of the East, the many wonderful things accomplished by the Three Kings in Cologne, unknown in this country, are found both in books and by word of mouth. They say that the star which stood over the town of Stulla, which lay under Mount Vaus before the death of the Three Kings, stands in these days immovable over Cologne. It is also written that a beautiful golden star like the one which shone for the Three Holy Kings on Christmas night and led them to Bethlehem, now stands before the coffin of the Three Holy Kings. They also say that the right arms of the Three Holy Kings at Cologne are decorated with costly stones, and in one king's hand is gold, in another incense and in the third myrrh, and that these arms are displayed on special pilgrimages; at such times, the holy legs are rubbed with gold and silver and from them exudes a priceless fragrance, better than the scent of any flower. It is also written that when the town of Cologne is stricken with trouble, a priest takes our Lord's Body, and three other priests with golden crowns on their heads each take an arm of the Three Holy Kings and cause a golden star made for the purpose to be carried before them, and so a procession is made through the town with music and ceremony, till they come to a special church chosen for the purpose. Then the Holy Sacrament with the arms of the Three Kings is placed on the altar, and at the appointed time the three crowned priests go to the altar and each takes an arm and offers it to the sacrament, one after the other, and in the hands of the arms are gold, incense and myrrh, and so our Lord forgets his wrath and releases the town of Cologne from its troubles.

The Indians further say that they still have in their town relics of Barlaam and Josaphat and other holy royal ancestors; the grave where the Three Holy Kings were first laid to rest is still unharmed and is visited and honoured by pilgrims from distant lands. We find too that Indians, who come to Jerusalem on business or to the Holy Sepulchre, buy finger rings from pilgrims from our country, which have been rubbed on the bones of the Three Holy Kings. The Indians hold these rings in high regard, and often kiss them with devotion, and say that many sick people have been healed by them. Occasionally pilgrims from our country are encountered in Jerusalem, who have brought with them jewels and other articles, such as small rings, mirrors, rosaries and purses, and say that they have brought them from Cologne. They also display earth from the churchyard of the Eleven Thousand Virgins at Cologne: these articles and the earth Indians and other Western people buy eagerly, for they say they suffer in many ways from the cry of frogs and other reptiles, but when this earth is scattered on the swamp, they can no longer hear the frogs. Many Indians who come to Jerusalem wish to be taken to Cologne, but they are afraid of the cold; still many set out on the way, but they either die on the journey or turn back again, for the Indians are not used to cold at home, but as soon as they leave their own land, they suffer frostbite, and put on furs made of the skins of the most costly animals, which reach the ankles, for the Indians are small people and have brown faces, and yet are clever and intelligent in many things. When they are in Jerusalem and hear about Cologne and the Three Holy Kings, they write it down straight away under their lord's seal, so that they can report it to Prester John when they return home. From all this, it is clear that the Three Kings are held in great honour through the whole of the East.

Chapter 46

So Cologne, honoured town, rejoice. God has sent to you his great treasure, with which he has celebrated so many wonders; rejoice that he has chosen and appointed you before all the towns of the world to possess the tomb of the Three Holy Kings. Should you not, therefore, turn to God and thank him, and give honour and praises to the Three Holy Kings, that you have been found worthy of so great a blessing.

Bibliography

Borenius/Tristram, *Englische Malerei des Mittelalters*, Schmidt & Günther, 1927.

Francis Cheetham, *English Mediaeval Alabasters*, Phaedon-Christies, 1984.

——, Article in 'Gothic Exports', *Antique Collector*, 1993.

William Dalrymple, *In Xanadu*, Flamingo, 1992.

Eamon Duffy, *The Stripping of the Altars*, Yale University Press, 1992.

Adrian G. Gilbert, *Magi*, Bloomsbury Publishing PLC, 1996.

Maurice Hasting, *St. Stephen's Chapel and its place in the development of the perpendicular style in England*, Cambridge, 1955.

F. S. Haydon (ed.), *Chronicon ... a monacho quodam Malmesburiensis*, Rolls Series, 1858.

W. L. Hildburgh, 'English Alabaster Tables' in *Art Bulletin*, 32, 1950.

Johannes von Hildesheim, Facsimile of Simrock's edition 1842, reprinted Omega Verlag, Kassel, 1979.

Hans Hofmann, *Die Heiligen Drei Könige*, Röhrscheid Verlag, Bonn, 1975.

C. Horstmann, *The Three Kings of Cologne*, E. E. Text Society, 1886.

Michael Molinar, *The Star of Bethlehem*, Rutgers University Press, 1990.

C. F. Pitman, 'Nottingham Alabaster Carvings' in the *Connoisseur*, 1954.

——, *Reflections on Nottingham Alabaster Carvings.*

Walter Schulten, *Der Schrein der Heiligen Drei Könige*, Luthe-Druck, Köln, 1975.

William of Newburgh, Yorkshire, *Historia Anglicana*, Rolls Series, (ed.) R. Howelett, 1884.

E. Carus Wilson, article in *Hanse in Europa*, Kölnisches Stadtmuseum, 1973.

H. Yule and H. Cordier, *The Book of Ser Marco Polo*, John Murray, 1902